D0945301

Hermann Hesse

by THEODORE ZIOLKOWSKI

Columbia University Press

NEW YORK *&* LONDON 1966

Hermann Hesse is Number 22 of the series

THEODORE ZIOLKOWSKI, Professor of German at Princeton University, is the author of *Hermann Broch* and *The Novels of Hermann Hesse.*

First printing 1966
Second printing 1969
Library of Congress Catalog Card Number: 66-26002
Printed in the United States of America

Passages from the published works of Hesse are quoted, in the author's own translation, by courtesy of Suhrkamp Verlag, Frankfurt am Main.

Hermann Hesse

Hermann Hesse's favorite pastimes were painting and gardening. We should bear this in mind. Or, better still, we should visualize the writer in his overalls, placidly burning weeds on a terraced slope or, palette in hand, gazing sharply from beneath a broad-brimmed hat at the radiant vistas of southern Switzerland. Since intellectually and linguistically Hesse is an heir of the chronic dualism that has afflicted German writers at least since Schiller, he tends quite casually to use such ear-filling generalities as Spirit and Nature, Intellect and Sense, Ideal and Reality, Art and Life, Yin and Yang. But if we remember the poet with his paint brush and spade, we can put the dialectical polarities into a more human perspective and lend substance to the heady abstractions.

Almost all Hesse's heroes are riven by this conflict. They are artists alienated from life, intellectuals who eye the senses warily; or, conversely, they are sober citizens unsettled by a vague longing for freedom, men disenchanted with reality who yearn for an ideal. The dialectical rhythm takes many forms. Hesse's earliest works affect a haughty aestheticism characteristic of the *fin de siècle*, but his first major novel, *Peter Camenzind*, represents a complete *volte-face* to a Rousseau-like return to nature. In such later works as *Demian* or *The Steppenwolf* the conflict is acted out within the soul of a single individual, while in *Narziss and Goldmund* the dual roles are assigned to two representative heroes. *Siddhartha* lays out the realms of

Sense and Intellect geographically in a symbolic landscape through which the hero passes; the protagonist of *The Glass Bead Game* is confronted with a choice between a *vita activa* and a *vita contemplativa*. But no matter how the dualism is expressed and no matter which way the pendulum seems to swing in individual works, everything goes back to the recluse in his garden, who is equally content pruning his bushes or trying to capture their beauty in pastels.

Let us take a closer look at Hesse's aquarelles, many of which illustrate autograph manuscripts of his poems and stories. Two basic types strike our eye. The first, more realistic ones spread out the semi-tropical landscape of the Ticino in bold, bright colors: planes are emphasized almost cubistically, silhouettes are marked with strong lines, the entire scene is reduced to its salient motifs. The setting is instantly recognizable, but it has been intensified, sharpened, enhanced by the craft of the painter. This heightened realism characterizes Hesse's prose as well. In his fiction as in his paintings the details that make for naturalism are effaced. The dialogue is not differentiated; the episodes stand out in haut-relief without the transitions that make for verisimilitude but add nothing to the essential meaning of the picture or plot. It is a realism that, at its best, borders on symbolism and, at its worst, flattens out into a pretentious allegory.

In the second category all pretense at realism is missing: human bodies sprout out of fantastic trees, flowers unfold faces, animals display blossoms instead of heads, lovely but undecipherable designs captivate the eye. This phantasy style distinguishes the many fairy tales that Hesse wrote after 1917. But it also dominates the grand visions of *Demian*, the Magic Theater of *The Steppenwolf*, the self-portrait of the painter Klingsor, and many scenes of *The Journey to the East*. Through such bold images Hesse expressed, in his painting as well as in his prose, the unity of all being that he envisages as the ultimate resolution of the conflict between Nature and Spirit, Reality and Ideal, and the other polarities.

We must not imagine that this resolution was the prerogative of Hesse the artist. In the idyll *Hours in the Garden* (1936) Hesse described with affectionate detail his daily routine, whose high point arrived when he heaped up the day's accumulation of rubbish, leaves, and dry twigs to burn. "For me, fire signifies an alchemistic-symbolic cult in the service of the divinity: the retransformation of multiplicity into the One." The language is ponderous, but the meaning is clear. Fire (as well as water—another medium of the gardener) enters his works frequently as an ontological symbol of the unification of opposites. Nature, Spirit, Unity—thesis, antithesis, synthesis—this is the rhythm of Hesse's works, but it is a rhythm that emerged first in his own life and for which his works provide the subsequent metaphors. It is easy to lose sight of this and to forget that an existential experience inevitably underlies the romantic abstractions of which Hesse was so fond. However tempting it may seem to establish neat theoretical schemes in order to explain Hesse's works, it is a danger to be avoided. For there is a constant delicate interaction between Hesse's life and his writings; the abstractions have no inherent validity, but only the significance that they receive from Hesse's own experiences. His scope as a writer was narrow because he was constantly obsessed with his own personality and its pendulation between Spirit and Nature, between painter and gardener. But his works display a grand imaginative sweep by virtue of Hesse's poetic ability to find ever new images, symbols, and structures through which to express what he conceived as man's basic dilemma.

Hesse was fond of saying that he decided to become a writer at the age of twelve or thirteen. Born in 1877 into a family of Protestant missionaries, he was destined to follow the academic path that led from his South German birthplace of Calw through the University of Tübingen to a life of spiritual service. Spirit and service ultimately came—they are central themes in his later works—but not exactly as his family had planned. From the start Hesse rebelled so vehemently against restraints at home that his parents toyed shamefacedly with the idea of sending him away to school. For twelve years they were able to cope with the headstrong boy—first in Calw, from 1881 to 1886 in Basel, and then again in Calw, where his father had taken over the Calw Missionary Press. (In many of his works it is this absurdly picturesque Black Forest town that provides the background for the narrative.)

By the time he was twelve, Hesse could no longer be handled at home. His family, as his father wrote, was "too nervous, too weak" to contend with his energies. So he was packed off to preparatory school in near-by Göppingen, where stern discipline went hand in hand with academic excellence in preparation for the dreaded regional board examinations that provided entry and tuition to one of the famous "seminaries" of Württemberg. During the year and a half at Göppingen, portrayed in the novel *The Prodigy*, Hesse applied himself so diligently that he was among the privileged few who passed the examinations in the summer of 1891, thus winning a place in the educational system that had produced a dynasty of Swabian intellectuals including Kepler, Hölderlin, and Hegel. Hesse entered school at Maulbronn, a beautifully preserved monastery that was later to provide the medieval setting for his novel *Narziss and Goldmund*. At first he responded enthusiastically to new friends and to the excellent classical education offered to the aspiring young theologians and academicians. But within a few months Hesse's old restlessness showed itself again. In March 1892 he ran away and had to be brought back, after a night in a haystack, by the forest patrol. This episode was the prelude to such a severe fit of depression that his parents withdrew him from school.

For the next few months the future Nobel Prize winner was sent from one institution to another. First his parents turned him over to a famous exorciser, who tried to pray him back to health, with the perhaps not surprising result that the troubled youth tried to commit suicide. Next he was sent to a home for weak-minded children where, as part of his rehabilitation, he worked in the garden and tutored less gifted classmates. After a third abortive attempt at a school in Basel, Hesse attended the *gymnasium* at Bad Cannstatt for a year, where he spent most of his time frequenting bars and piling up debts—a period of despondency and profligacy recounted in the fourth chapter of *Demian*. By this time Hesse's parents realized as clearly as he that formal education was not for him. In October 1893 he contracted as a bookdealer's apprentice in Esslingen, but after three days ran away again and returned to Calw, where for half a year he did little but embarrass his family by his presence. From June 1894 to September 1895 Hesse settled down to the rather dull job of filing gears as a mechanic's apprentice in the Calw Tower Clock Factory, an experience that was to pay off in his early stories by giving him a sympathetic insight into the mentality of small-town workers and apprentices.

Finally Hesse seemed to find himself. Again he signed on as an apprentice bookdealer—this time in the university town of Tübingen—and actually managed to remain in the position for the four years necessary to receive his apprentice's letter. At last his dream of becoming a writer began to materialize in more than his unorthodox behavior. His poems were accepted from time to time by journals and newspapers. He found a coterie of compatible friends who styled themselves the *petit cénacle* and posed for group photographs lying, in Wildean lassitude, before *Jugendstil* backgrounds. During these same years he began the broad reading that eventually produced, besides the impressive monograph "A Little Library of World Literature," scores of essays on writers and books. But though his reading was often sturdy—Goethe was a favorite—his own efforts remained rather precious. The poems published in his first volume, *Romantic Songs* (1899), feature languishing poets who loll in the fragrant night listening to lovely ladies playing Chopin nocturnes on grand pianos.

A second product of the Tübingen years was the series of misty prose poems entitled *An Hour beyond Midnight* (1899) and clearly indebted to Maeterlinck. By this title Hesse hoped to adumbrate "the dreamland of my creative hours and days, which lay mysteriously somewhere between time and space." These *poèmes en prose* sought to create "an artist's dreamworld, an isle of beauty; its poetic character was a retreat from the storms and depressions of the everyday world into night, dream and lovely solitude." Though his Pietist parents were probably gratified that the *enfant perdu* was beginning to support himself and to attain a certain success as a writer, they could not have been much comforted by such letters as the one in which he wrote: "For a long time I have had the firm conviction that morality is replaced, for artists, by aesthetics." His spiritual mentor, of course, was Nietzsche, who peered down at the young poet from two pictures on the walls of his sparsely furnished room. His aesthetic idol was Chopin, whom Hesse found "noble in every respect, though often degenerate."

The dialectical rhythm asserted itself when Hesse left Tübingen in 1899 to work in a bookshop in Basel—for him the home of Nietzsche, Jacob Burckhardt, and Arnold Böcklin. In one of his first letters he wrote: "The period of Romanticism is over." His work-in-progress, *The Posthumous Writings and Poems of Hermann Lauscher* (1901), was a conscious attempt "to conquer for myself a piece of world and reality." Written under the impact of the most realistic of German Romantics–E. T. A. Hoffmann–it sought to look objectively, even ironically, at the years of his literary *bohème*. The work was impressive enough to interest S. Fischer, the enterprising publisher who was building up one of Germany's most exciting presses. Hesse sent Fischer the manuscript of his next novel, which exchanged the perfumed hazes of his early poems and prose for the invigorating *plein-air* of the Swiss Alps, which Hesse had discovered since his arrival in Basel. *Peter Camenzind* (1904) was an immediate success that brought Hesse international recognition, prizes, and–not least–his first financial independence. Peter Camenzind, in many respects a literary descendant of Gottfried Keller's Green Henry, is a Swiss peasant boy who attains fame as a writer and succumbs for a time to the glamour of the city with its *salons* and intellectual attractions. But ultimately he renounces the empty freedom of aestheticism and returns to his village in the Alps for a life of modest responsibility.

In Hesse's biography life reveals a pronounced tendency to imitate art. After the success of *Peter Camenzind* he married Marie Bernoulli, who might easily have stepped out of one of his early poems. Nine years older than Hesse, she played Schumann and Chopin beautifully and loved nothing better than melancholy solitude. The couple rented a peasant house on the shore of Lake Constance and settled down to a life of what Hesse envisaged as rustic familial bliss. On the surface things went well; the eight years in Gaienhofen were immensely productive in a number of ways. Following the pattern of vaguely melancholy realism established in *Peter Camenzind*, he turned out dozens of stories and poems about little people—shopkeepers, apprentices, tramps—that were incorporated into commercially successful volumes with such titles as *In This World* (1907), *Neighbors* (1908), *On the Road* (1911), and *By-Ways* (1912)—a far cry from the romantic poems and timeless-spaceless dimensions of his first efforts. In *The Prodigy* (1906)—a school novel of the type being produced in those years by Rilke, Robert Musil, and others—he reassessed the anguish of the uncertain years surrounding Maulbronn, showing how easily he himself, like his hero Hans Giebenrath, might have ended in suicide. The novel *Gertrude* (1910) reflects the company he kept in Gaienhofen; for though he received occasional visits from fellow writers, Hesse preferred to associate with musicians and painters. The hero of *Gertrude*, which bears a strong resemblance to *Tonio Kröger* and other early works by Thomas Mann, is a crippled musician whose art prevents him from achieving happiness in life, a spiritual affliction symbolized by his physical disability.

Stimulated by trips to Italy, Hesse wrote biographical studies of Boccaccio and St. Francis of Assisi. He prepared popular editions of lyric poetry and romantic authors and reviewed scores of books. He was a frequent contributor to the satirical weekly *Simplicissimus* as well as one of the founding editors of the liberal-oppositional journal *März*. And three sons were born, who played about him happily as he worked in his garden. Fortune smiled brightly upon the bespectacled young man who, only a few years earlier, had been standing behind the counter of a bookstore in Basel.

But external circumstances are deceptive. While he was leading the life glorified in his books, Hesse was chafing inwardly. He felt that he was rapidly vegetating in the "land of the Philistines" that he heartily detested. Squatting in his garden, he asked himself uneasily if he was not really more of a nomad than a planter. This tension between security and

Wanderlust betrayed itself in the ever more frequent lecture tours that took him away from Gaienhofen for weeks at a time. When the trips to Italy, the lectures in Germany, Austria, and Switzerland no longer satisfied this nomadic urge, Hesse embarked in 1911 on a voyage to India.

The Orient had long represented an ideal in Hesse's mind. His grandfather Hermann Gundert had spent over two decades as a missionary in India and was the author of many scholarly works on the East. His father, Johannes Hesse, had worked in Mangalur for four years before poor health necessitated his return to Europe. The Pietist Mission House in Calw, where Hesse spent the most impressionable years of his childhood, entertained a constant stream of visitors heading for India or coming from there. "From the time I was a child," Hesse wrote, "I breathed in and absorbed the spiritual side of India just as deeply as Christianity." It was inevitable that the nomadic impulse that lured him in ever-widening gyres away from the bourgeois security of Gaienhofen should ultimately lead him to India. "We come to the South and East full of longing, driven by a dark and grateful premonition of home, and we find here a paradise. We find the pure, simple, childlike people of paradise." But Hesse had failed to reckon with the problematics of his own nature, which could not be cast off so easily as his European overcoat. "We ourselves are different; we are alien here and without any rights of citizenship. We lost our paradise long ago, and the new one that we wish to build is not to be found along the equator and on the warm seas of the East. It lies within us and in our own northern future." Though the trip to India bore fruit ten years later in the "Indic Poem" *Siddhartha*, it was initially a disappointment. Hesse still did not realize that his flights into the world were not flights from Gaienhofen, but flights from himself.

Shortly after his return to Europe, he attempted to alleviate his restlessness by moving from the isolation of Gaienhofen to the more urban atmosphere of Bern. In *Rosshalde*, the last major work of these prewar years, Hesse posed the question that he had not yet dared to ask in reality: Is a happy marriage conceivable for an artist, for a man "who not only lives by his instincts, but who—above all—wishes to observe and depict as objectively as possible?" In the novel the answer is no. The painter Veraguth is so wholly committed to his art that the only tenuous bond still linking him to his wife is their son Pierre. They have a brief moment of closeness when their son falls ill with cerebral meningitis, that symbolic disease that plays a role in many artist-novels (for example, Thomas Mann's *Doctor Faustus* and Aldous Huxley's *Point Counter Point*) because it afflicts precisely those senses of sight and sound so important to the artist. When Pierre dies, their marriage has no further justification. "All that he had left was his art, of which he had never been so assured as now. All that he had left was the solace of the outsider, to whom it is not given to seize life and drink it to the dregs." It was two more years before Hesse, still imitating his own art, was forced to a similar conclusion.

His most popular work in the years before his crisis was a series of three stories revolving around *Knulp* (1915). Here, in a lighthearted form with undertones of tragedy, Hesse approaches the problem of nomad versus planter, bourgeois versus artist, from another point of view. Knulp is a lovable vagabond who wanders from town to town, staying with friends who regard it as a privilege to feed and shelter the happy ne'er-do-well, but consistently refuses to tie himself down to any one of the many trades at which he has an instinctive facility. At the end of his life, as he lies dying in a snowstorm, Knulp has an interview with God in which he reproaches himself for his wasted life. God explains that it had been the whole purpose of Knulp's life to bring "a little nostalgia for freedom" into the lives of ordinary men. So Knulp dies with a contented smile. But hidden beneath the light surface of the three stories is the guilty conscience of the artist who suspects that his life and freedom are worthless, even immoral. This is the quandary of Hesse's early heroes. Veraguth longs for freedom and feels restricted by his marriage and family responsibilities, while Knulp's enjoyment of his freedom is tempered by his feeling that he should do something worthwhile for society.

World War I shattered the last vestiges of the happy idyll that Hesse had tried to build in the years following *Peter Camenzind*. Unlike most Europeans, he did not share the now almost incomprehensible elation at the birth of a new era that characterized the public reaction to the outbreak of the war. In a series of essays he exhorted his countrymen and foreigners alike to pacifism, to a spirit of transcendent internationalism, to a grand humanism; and he reaped only scorn and vituperation for his efforts. The best-selling author was now branded publicly as "a viper nourished at the breast" of an unsuspecting audience. For a time Hesse worked selflessly in the local internment camps and edited books, journals, and newspapers for distribution to German prisoners-of-war in other countries. Then in 1916, his father died; his son Martin became seriously ill; and his wife suffered such a severe nervous disorder that she had to be put into a sanatorium. Hesse's marriage and family had disintegrated. Life was catching up with art. But unlike his hero Veraguth, who had at least the consolation of his art, Hesse had lost faith even in his writing. When he was asked, a few years later, to prepare an edition of his Selected Works, he refused: "There was nothing there to select. . . . There was no doubt in my mind that, of all my stories, not a single one was good enough as a work of art to be worth mentioning."

Hesse was saved as a man and restored as a writer by the intensive self-scrutiny precipitated by psychoanalysis. As the result of a nervous breakdown, he undertook in 1916 and 1917 a series of consultations with Josef B. Lang, a disciple of Jung, in a sanatorium near Lucerne. Lang, who became a close friend and crops up in Hesse's letters and narratives under the pseudonyms "Longus" and "Pistorius," introduced Hesse to the writings of Freud and Jung and helped him with the systematic analysis of his problematic mentality. Lang's own notebooks indicate that he received much, in turn, from Hesse, who greeted psychoanalysis not as a radically new invention, but rather as the systematization of instinctive knowledge long present in the works of his favorite writers. In any case, Hesse perceived that his ever more frantic flights, in the years 1904 to 1914, had been flights from himself, projections into the outer world of his own torments. And his writing had been correspondingly subjective. "All these stories dealt with me, reflected my own path, my own secret dreams and wishes, my own bitter anguish." Renouncing his mandarin pose of detachment, he proclaimed his own complicity in the events of a world gone insane: "I am farther from all Truth than ever before. . . . But I feel that I am alive again, younger, I sense a future."

The immediate product of this rebirth was the novel *Demian*, written in a few hectic weeks of 1917. *Demian* is the probing account of a young man's search for personal values, his quest for identity, and thus a supratemporal, almost mythic tale. At the same time, it is dated to the extent that it is a response to the specific needs of the youth of World War I, a generation that Hesse—now forty years old—viewed with an objectivity lacking in his earlier works. Hesse himself was a bitter opponent of the war. Yet through the figure of his hero he attempted to explain the mystical fervor with which the youth of 1914 greeted the outbreak of the war as the beginning of a new era. Hesse was always an outsider. Yet in the novel he presents the appeal of community and the solace of solidarity. Inasmuch as Hesse exploits these and other factors—the rebellion against the father, the messianic belief in a new humanity, the evangelical rhetoric of language—it can be argued that the novel is a response to and an interpretation of the generation of expressionism. This explains the immense appeal of the novel, which rapidly captured an entirely new group of readers for its author.

At the same time, it is a deeply personal book, tracing symbolically in the life of a much younger man Hesse's own development during the period of his psychoanalysis. The hero of the first-person narrative, Emil Sinclair, recounts certain crucial episodes from his life between ten and twenty. Sinclair's boyhood revolves around his ambivalent friendship with Max Demian. When he goes off to boarding school he slumps at first into profligacy. But the ethereal love he conceives for a girl he glimpses in the park and the mystical pronouncements of a new friend, the renegade theologian Pistorius, gradually steady his uncertainties. At the university he meets Demian again and enters into an ambiguous relationship with his friend's mother, Frau Eva. This year of happiness is ended by the war, which soon claims Demian as a victim, but leads Sinclair to the final stage of spiritual independence in which he no longer has need of external mentors.

Hesse's own vacillation between the two imagined poles of being is introduced in the first chapter as the "Two Worlds" of which Sinclair becomes aware. At home, in the harmonious security of his father's house, Sinclair has grown up in a "light" world of order and Christian ethics. But when he goes down to the servants' quarters or, on the streets, sees drunks being hauled off to jail, he perceives the existence of a "dark" world—a world of sex, violence, lust—which is wholly denied by his parents and toward which the boy Sinclair feels himself ineluctably attracted. For he senses, with the first stirrings of puberty, that this "dark" world, rejected so disdainfully by his family, is no less a natural part of life than their own artificially rationalized "light" world. At first Sinclair wavers back and forth between the two worlds of his experience, finding satisfaction in neither. With the aid of Demian, he discovers that he longs inchoately for a new deity, an ideal embracing both worlds: "a god who also encompasses within himself the devil, and before whom one wouldn't need to close one's eyes in shame when the most natural things in the world go on." The novel is the story of this search for a new deity, a search that leads Sinclair from one teacher to another until, transcending them all, he discovers a new source of values within himself.

Even this brief sketch of the novel's theme reveals something about the strengths and weaknesses of Hesse's mature prose and helps to explain the ambiguous feelings it arouses in his readers. For the rejection of established values, the search for personal identity, the need for moral commitment—these are essentially modern themes that anticipate the mood of our own midcentury. But in Hesse's works these themes are radically internalized, producing an essentially lyrical fiction in which the customary attributes of the novel as we have grown to know it are missing.

In *Demian* the theme is reflected in a form and language largely determined by religious symbols. The episodes of Sinclair's life are patterned explicitly on Christian motifs and metaphors. His expeditions into the "dark" world are related to the parable of the Prodigal Son, and he looks back longingly at the security of his parents' world as at "a lost paradise." Sinclair, Demian, and the others who rebel against the world of their fathers bear "the Mark of Cain," and they feel more sympathy for the unrepentant thief than for the third man on the cross who "celebrates lugubrious festivals of betterment and remorse." Sinclair is first thrust out of the paradise of his childhood because he claims to have stolen forbidden apples; his acceptance of the new deity is related in a chapter entitled "The Struggle with the Angel."

The two central symbols of the book are likewise religious. The bird breaking its way out of an egg—an image of spiritual rebirth that recurs constantly from the first page to the last—is borrowed, by way of Bachofen, from late Roman cultism. Here, of course, the symbol has been redefined to correspond to the theme of the novel. The egg represents the dualistic world that insists on arbitrary distinctions between good and evil, a world that must be shattered if a new reality is to be formed. And Abraxas, the god of good and evil to whom Sinclair is introduced by Demian and Pistorius, is a central Gnostic deity. Mother Eva, finally, is a Christian archetype colored by the Jungian conception of *anima*. With her son Demian she anticipates the hermaphroditic goal of unification in which the tensions of the novel are ultimately resolved.

This play with religious forms, which shapes both the language and the structure of the novel, does not merely reflect the path of Sinclair's development. It also provides the background for the key figure, Demian himself. For only within such an ironically religious framework do we realize that Demian is a Christ figure. The illumination of his forehead, his "miracles," his teaching by parables, his belief in a new kingdom, his band of disciples—all these traits, taken singly as they are scattered through the novel, might easily be overlooked. But within the symbolic framework they coalesce to constitute the image of a modern Christ, but ironically, since his teaching is anything but Christian.

At this point we begin to comprehend the basic unity of the novel. A first-person narrative about a Christ written by a devoted disciple is known as a gospel, and *Demian* has all the characteristics of a gospel—the travesty of a gospel! Just as the novel represents structurally a reshaping of common Christian myths, it constitutes thematically a revaluation of Christian ideas. The theme of *Demian* is essentially Nietzschean. But for Hesse, as he has repeatedly stated, Christ and Nietzsche are not contradictory but complementary: they are both outstanding examples, in the history of mankind, of the individual search for personal values. In this search they are allied, though the formalization of their systems may cause them to seem far apart.

Demian was published in 1919 under the pseudonym of Emil Sinclair. Hesse was striving for the effect of authenticity. But, above all, he did not wish to be identified with what he now called his "sentimental-bourgeois" works, whose validity he had begun to question and whose appeal to the generation of *Demian* he rightfully doubted. The deception was so nearly complete that the book was awarded the Fontane Prize for first novels. It was almost a year before the mask was lifted; Hesse returned the prize. But he had succeeded in freeing himself from the stigma of his own reputation and in capturing a new audience. Though his subsequent works were published under his own name, he continued, around the end of World War I, to use the pseudonym Sinclair for a series of essays addressed to the younger generation. In the most characteristic of these, entitled "Self Reliance" (*Eigensinn*), he justifies reflectively the theme of personal values that he had treated fictionally in *Demian*. "There is one virtue that I particularly love: Self Reliance. All the other popular and praised virtues represent obedience to laws handed down by men. Only Self Reliance does not ask about these laws. He who is self reliant obeys another law, a single and absolutely sacred law: the law within himself, his own law."

Another of these essays, "Zarathustra's Return," is written in conscious, and skillful, imitation of Nietzsche's hymnic style. As the crowds of young admirers swarm around him, disappointed that he offers them no facile solutions to the problems of life, Zarathustra smiles: "Behold, Zarathustra is not a teacher. . . . Zarathustra has seen much, he has suffered much. But only one thing has he learned, only one thing constitutes his wisdom, only one thing is his pride. He has learned to be Zarathustra. You should learn to be yourselves, just as I have learned to be Zarathustra." This is a refrain that Hesse was to echo in hundreds of letters to readers who approached him for touchstones of conduct. His works, he insists, are not examples to be followed specifically, but only models of lives that question reality in an attempt to find the private solution. The questions may be the same for every man, but the answers vary from individual to individual. "Loneliness is the way," he continues, "by which destiny leads man to himself."

Loneliness was the course that Hesse now chose. In the isolated village of Montagnola, above the valley of Lugano, he found the surroundings in which he was to spend the remainder of his life. During the summer of 1919, in a great surge of activity, he wrote several important essays, two of his finest novellas, and he discovered the avocation that was to bring him rich hours of contentment in years to come: painting. The external restlessness that had marked his life until 1914 was sublimated. From this time on his problematic quest is wholly internalized. Instead of being wasted on fruitless expeditions through the world outside, it is concentrated into works of a new quality that differ, by their intensity and control, from the older works as much as the Hesse of Montagnola differs from the young householder of Gaienhofen. In a certain sense it might be said that Hesse ceases to be merely contemporary and becomes modern. Although his early writings anticipate in many individual points his later ones, the early books rarely transcend the level of considerable talent, whereas the works after 1917 place him often in the company of the finest writers of the twentieth century.

Despite all superficial differences, *Klein and Wagner* and *Klingsor's Last Summer* are complementary works. They are Hesse's two longest–and finest–novellas. In both, the action is compressed geographically and temporally into a brief period and into a Southern landscape that reflect Hesse's own life in the summer of 1919. Both have heroes who are forty-two (Hesse's age at the time of composition) and thus notably older than the heroes of his earlier tales. And in both the hero's death is preceded by a grand vision of unity in which the polarities of life are resolved.

Friedrich Klein is more than an autobiographical mask. He exemplifies the guilty conscience of many literati of the twentieth century who regard their way of life as somewhat illicit, if not downright criminal. (This symbolic consciousness raises Hesse's mature work above the merely private and relates it to the thematics of contemporaries like Thomas Mann, Hermann Broch, or André Gide, in whose writings the equation "artist = criminal" also plays a central role.) Klein is an embezzler. After a lifetime of sobriety as a reliable clerk, a steady husband, and a devoted father, he has absconded with a huge sum, deserted wife and children, and fled to the South under the assumed name of Wagner. But Klein finds no immediate pleasure in his new, illicit freedom. He is convinced, to be sure, that his previous life was a false one, modeled more after the expectations and demands of his wife than after his own wishes. For her sake he had subdued the "criminal," adventurous side of his nature. Yet certain bourgeois traits are so firmly ingrained in his character that he is disconcerted by the provocative glance of a pretty blonde wearing bright lipstick and shoes with stiletto heels.

It was Hesse who penned the title *Klein and Wagner;* in his own mind Klein poses the question as Klein *or* Wagner. Klein (which means "small" in German) represents the bourgeois side of his personality; the artistic, "criminal" part he calls Wagner. This refers not only to Richard Wagner as a symbol of overriding artistry, but also to a *cause célèbre* of the years just before the war: the case of the psychopathic schoolteacher Ernst Wagner, who murdered his wife and four children. Klein, as a child, had always hated his name, which seemed to epitomize the pettiness of his life. "Wagner was the murderer and the fugitive within him; but Wagner was also the composer, the artist, the genius, the seducer, the inclination to *joie de vivre*, sensual pleasure, luxury." Klein-Wagner's malaise stems from his inability to reconcile what he regards as the two contradictory poles of his personality. Thus, in the main episode of the novella, he is both attracted and repelled by the dancer Teresina, who personifies the sensuality that he had always longed for and yet feared.

By the end of a week he manages to overcome his inhibitions and rise to the heights of the illicit passion of his imagination. Yet, when he awakes that night from bad dreams and peers down at Teresina's nude beauty, he reverts to his bourgeois abhorrence of sensuality and seizes a knife in order to kill her. He comes to his senses at the last moment and, horrified by what he had almost done, flees from the house and rows out to the middle of the lake. As he sits there, his legs dangling in the water, he reflects on the implications of the philosophical imperative: to let oneself go. Translating Schopenhauer's thought into action, he sinks into the dark waters and, in a great vision, sees the poles of his being not as contradictory, but as parts of a greater whole. "The whole secret was: to let oneself go! If he had done that a single time, if he had succumbed, surrendered, yielded himself; if he had renounced all supports and all firm ground underneath. If he listened only to the guide in his own heart, then everything was won, everything was all right: no longer any fear, no longer any danger." At this point of awareness, of course, his suicide becomes meaningless. But since, by a logical extension, life and death are also one and the same, further life becomes irrelevant as well. So Klein-Wagner dies in total surrender to the water that so often plays the symbolic role of unification in Hesse's works.

Klein and Wagner is a tightly constructed novella that bears detailed comparison with such masterpieces of the genre as Thomas Mann's *Death in Venice*. *Klingsor's Last Summer*, by contrast, is a loose series of sketches tied together only by their painter-hero. Thematically the two works are close: the final vision of an all-encompassing unity revealed to the drowning Klein is paralleled here in the Chagall-like self portrait that Klingsor paints just before his own death.

"He saw many, many faces behind his own face in the large mirror framed by stupid rose vines, and he painted them into his picture: the sweet and astonished faces of children, the foreheads of young men filled with dreams and fire, scornful drunkard's eyes, thirsting lips. . . . And not his face alone, or his thousand faces were painted into this portrait, not merely his own eyes and lips. He also painted hordes of naked women, driven past like birds in a storm, sacrificial offerings to the idol Klingsor, and a youth with the face of suicide, distant temples and forests. . . ."

But whereas the scenes in *Klein and Wagner* are tempered gloomily by the uneasy conscience of Klein, whose feelings of guilt cast a pall upon the very landscape, the atmosphere in *Klingsor's Last Summer* is radiant with the beauty that Hesse, wandering around the Ticino with his camp stool and palette, had begun to discover in the world. These stories provide a perfect example for what Ralph Freedman has analyzed as the lyrical quality of Hesse's fiction; the external reality—which is identical in both cases—is so disposed as to reflect the discrepant inner moods of the two heroes. Both works together constitute the entirety of Hesse's own vision: the schizophrenic rapture and depression of Klein along with the euphorious intoxication of Klingsor.

The theoretical background for the visions of unity in which the two novellas culminate is supplied by two important essays on Dostoevsky that Hesse wrote in 1919 and that, peripherally at least, entered English literature through T. S. Eliot's notes to *The Waste Land.* (Eliot was so deeply impressed by *In Sight of Chaos*—the collective title of the essays—that he made a trip to Montagnola to visit Hesse.) In "The Brothers Karamazov or the Decline of Europe" Hesse projects onto the scale of cultural history the conflict between "Two Worlds" that was still largely private in *Demian.* The pure "light" world, clinging desperately to a system of order that depends on the categorical rejection of certain attitudes defined arbitrarily as "bad," is represented by European Man. Opposed to this position, which is no longer tenable in the face of the relativism emerging in every area of modern science and philosophy, is Russian Man, personified by Dostoevsky's Karamazovs. Their ideal is "the departure from all established ethics and morality in favor of an attempt to understand everything, to accept everything." Unwilling to make absolute distinctions between good and evil, right and wrong, Russian Man worships a God who is at the same time Satan. (Here we see clearly an extension of Abraxas in *Demian.*) As this new spirit gradually permeates the West, the decline of traditional Graeco-Roman, Judaeo-Christian Europe becomes imminent.

From the standpoint of European Man, this "Russian" attitude seems criminal, a view that accounts for the criminal symbolism of *Klein and Wagner*. But simple awareness of the "criminal" impulses within us, the "chaos" of our souls, suffices; it is not necessary to proceed to the criminal act. Hesse demands merely that the New Man, confronted with—or abandoned by—a deity who will not prescribe our decisions by handing down convenient tables of law, should take upon himself the burden of this freedom and the responsibility of choice in a pluralistic world. The "decline of Europe" will be no violent upheaval, but an inner revolution: "the re-interpretation of worn-out symbols, the transvaluation of spiritual values." Hesse advocates a new morality linked closely to the attitudes advanced in the essay on "Self Reliance." Instead of cringing in despair or, like Klein, being driven to suicide by the apparent discrepancies between vision and reality, we should greet the breakdown of values as an occasion to assert ourselves in freedom as individuals. (If such thoughts sound familiar, it is because they anticipate in many respects the humanistic existentialism of our own day.)

"Thoughts on Dostoevsky's Idiot" offers a solution to the dilemma outlined in the first essay. Myshkin, the hero of the novel, is misunderstood and feared by his friends because his manner of seeing reality differs so radically from theirs. Whereas they are European Men, clinging to the values of a defunct system, he accepts all of life as it thrusts itself upon him. Especially during certain visionary moments (his epileptic seizures) he has stood at the magical boundary where all opposites are canceled out. As long as we remain within the framework of traditional reality, we see life in terms of clashing opposites. If we can step outside the system, only for a moment, it becomes evident that these apparent opposites actually constitute complementary parts of a greater whole. Magical Thinking is Hesse's rather romantic term for the act of mental projection that permits us to escape the sphere of polarities: it is a spiritual revaluation of life, proceeding from an uncompromising examination of the chaos in our own souls. The very opposite of anarchy, Magical Thinking implies the acknowledgment of a meaningful totality beyond chaos, for chaos is "chaotic" in a pejorative sense only from the standpoint of traditional concepts of order, of *fas* and *nefas*.

Such thoughts as these, outlined here and in other essays, explain why such ontological symbols of unity as fire and water and grand culminating visions play a central role in Hesse's works. In the fairy tales (*Märchen*) that he wrote during these years he renders symbolically the various processes of transformation through which unity and totality can be expressed. In "Pictor's Metamorphoses," for instance, the hero is transformed into a stone, a tree, a bird—images for the identity of all being. But even in his less fanciful fiction, unity is expressed in similar symbols and visions. *Demian* translated the Gnostic god Abraxas into a modern symbol of synthesis; *Klingsor's Last Summer* rendered the unification of all extremes in the artist's self-portraits. Like *Klein and Wagner*, Hesse's next novel *Siddhartha* (1922) culminates in an epiphany of unity when the hero peers into the river and sees mirrored there thousands of images that inundate his own reflection.

Siddhartha is a novel of classical symmetry, a perfection achieved, it might be added, at the cost of naturalness. Instead of style, it approaches stylization; instead of symbolism, allegory; instead of characterization, typology. Like Emil Sinclair, Siddhartha experiences the duality of nature and spirit before he finds the synthesis in a higher unity. But instead of vacillating between the impulses of his own personality, he finds the realms of Spirit and Nature spread out geographically upon a symbolic landscape in the India of Buddha.

The son of a Brahman, Siddhartha discovers at eighteen that

the religion of his father does not offer him the peace he seeks. So he sets out with his friend Govinda in search of the divine Atman. His first venture leads him away from the river of his birth to the ascetic Samanas, who cultivate the mind to the total exclusion of the senses. Gradually it becomes clear to Siddhartha that spirit alone cannot fulfil his expectations. Leaving Govinda among the followers of Buddha, he returns to the river and crosses into the land of the senses where he tarries for twenty years in the company of the courtesan Kamala, becoming a fat and prosperous businessman. At forty, however, Siddhartha realizes that sensual gratification has brought him no closer to happiness than pure intellect and spirit. He goes back to the river, which flows between the two symbolic worlds, joining them in its fluidity, and becomes the humble helper of the ferryman Vasudeva. For twenty more years he remains with Vasudeva the sage, learning not so much from his teaching as by his example that the true road to happiness is complete affirmation of all being, of *both* realms. As Hesse explained later: "*Siddhartha* glorifies not cognition, but love; it rejects dogma and revolves around the experience of unity."

In this novel Hesse's experience of India in 1911 reached fruition. The book should not be read as a glorification of Buddhism. In a diary note from 1920 Hesse stated categorically that he opposed Buddhism to the extent that it attempted to establish a fixed pattern of development—the Eightfold Path —just as he opposed any rigid religious dogma. It is, rather, a glorification of the man Buddha, who went his way just as doggedly as Christ and Nietzsche and whose life provides still another example of the qualities that Hesse admired above all others: self-reliance and rugged independence.

Here more than in any of Hesse's other works the inner vision has shaped external reality. The abstract concepts of spirit and nature wholly determine the Indian landscape of the book: The land of the Samanas is arid, while the land of Kamala is lush and verdant. The representatives of each geographical sphere are rigidly predetermined by their symbolic function in the novel: the Samanas never cross into the realm of the senses, and Kamala is able to go no further toward the Spirit than to the bank of the river. The language in the novel is equally stylized. Lacking the mystical rhetoric of *Demian* or the expressionistically fervent exuberance of *Klingsor*, it flows along with a paratactic smoothness that reflects the symmetry of the total structure. Siddhartha spends twenty years (his youth) in the realm of spirit; twenty more years among the "child-people" of the senses; and then twenty years on the synthesizing river before he finds his inner sense of unity. A taut discipline holds the novel together, just as Siddhartha's face—in the final vision—contains within it the seething masses of all humanity as beneath a thin film.

Siddhartha is an aesthetic *tour de force*, and its virtuosity stems from a concentrated effort to offset certain difficulties inherent in the theme. "My Indic poem got along splendidly as long as I was writing what I myself had experienced. . . . When I had finished with Siddhartha the Sufferer and wished to portray Siddhartha as a Victor, an Affirmer, a Subjugator—I couldn't go on." Again we sense the dialectical tension that underlies all of Hesse's works. Attempting to depict an ultimate synthesis that he himself had not attained, Hesse was forced to compensate for experience with an aesthetic structure that strains the potentialities of the genre. The resulting lyrical novel has an undeniable poetic beauty, perhaps the greatest that Hesse achieved; but it has equally undeniable shortcomings as fiction.

The year that followed the liberating euphoria of 1919 was "probably the most unproductive of my life, and thus the saddest," Hesse notes in his diary, and this is borne out by the difficulties in the composition of *Siddhartha*. After the completion of the novellas and the major essays, he killed time with other activities. From 1919 to 1922 he edited *Vivos Voco*, a journal devoted to the moral reconstruction of Europe. He wrote a number of minor essays, translated medieval Latin tales into German, and edited works of his favorite writers: Jean Paul, Novalis, Hölderlin, and others. Cut off from his family and former friends, he saw few people during these years except his future biographer, the Dadaist poet Hugo Ball, and Ruth Wenger, to whom he was married for a few months in 1924. Depressed by postwar developments in Germany, he became a Swiss citizen in 1923. For several grim years Hesse sat on his mountain in Switzerland, trying to come to terms with himself. His life again had not caught up with his art. It was 1924 before Hesse, like the Zarathustra of his own essay, persuaded himself to descend to the marketplace.

Forced to take a cure for rheumatic pains, Hesse began visiting the well-known spa of Baden outside Zürich. For the first time since his voluntary exile he found himself thrust into the midst of a society not of his own choosing. The unexpected result was the emergence of a sense of humor. Although some of his early stories had been imbued with a certain melancholy humor, Hesse's works after 1917 were grimly serious. *Demian*, *Siddhartha*, *In Sight of Chaos*, these are the products of a mind obsessed with grave problems and wholly unrelieved by the airiness of humor. They present ideal visions that are not open to question or doubt. Hesse's flight into solitude in 1919 was in part a flight from the necessity of confronting this ideal with the reality of the world around him. By 1924, however, the confrontation had become inevitable, and Hesse was forced to concede that reality bore little resemblance to the visions so sincerely outlined in his novels and essays. If he was to survive outside the hermetic isolation of Montagnola, he had to find a means of mediating between Reality and Ideal. This is essentially the subject of two long autobiographical essays *At the Spa* (1925) and *The Nuremberg Journey* (1927).

At the Spa, published originally under the title *Psychologia Balnearia* (1924), is inspired formally, as are many of Hesse's works, by the writings of the German romantics: in this case, by Jean Paul, the great humorist of romanticism. (There is another conspicuous parallel: Thomas Mann's *The Magic Mountain*, which appeared that same year. Although there are vast formal differences between the essay and the lengthy *Bildungsroman*, they share the abstracted setting of a health resort, the pervasive humor and the symbolic parallel between art and disease.) Here for the first time Hesse sensed the humorous possibilities of his dialectical sense of life. "We spa guests at Baden are especially in need of that knowledge of the antinomies: the stiffer our bones become, all the more urgently we require an elastic, two-sided, bipolar way of thinking."

During his psychoanalysis Hesse had come to acknowledge the relativism of all concepts. But it had not yet occurred to him to draw the final conclusion that this very relativism was in itself relative, that his view of life was meaningless to such ebullient types as the Dutch burgher in the adjoining room, who disturbed Hesse constantly with the earthy sounds of his living (another startling parallel to *The Magic Mountain* and Mijnheer Peeperkorn). The paean of incredulous distaste written about the Dutchman is a humorous effervescence worthy of Thomas Wolfe, a writer Hesse later admired. But the meaning of the episodes is deeper, for the noisy neighbor becomes for Hesse a symbol of the reality that he had to accept with love and humor: "My task was quite clear: I had to do away with my worthless hatred, I had to love the Dutchman. Then let him spit and bellow; I was superior to him, I was safe.

If I succeeded in loving him, then all his healthiness, all his vitality could not longer help him. Then he would be mine, then his image could no longer resist the idea of unity." This was not easy, and—in anticipation of the hero of his next novel—he often longed for his "home in the steppes." But by the time he was well enough to leave the spa, he had realized that humor is the only way to survive the otherwise tragic clash between reality and ideal. (When Hesse uses the word humor, it is always in the sense of German romanticism, where it connotes irony.)

Hesse's attitude has shifted and grown more complex. He no longer feels an apocalyptic rage or indignation about discordant aspects of life, but seeks to incorporate them with ironic understanding into his vision of unity. (This is especially true of *The Steppenwolf*, which has as its milieu the cocktail lounges and jazz bars of the 'twenties, which Hesse abhorred.) And he envisages a more sophisticated style, in which the "two worlds" of *Demian*, the two realms of *Siddhartha* will no longer be separated in an artificial dichotomy, but delicately intermingled as they occur in reality. He wishes that he had the counterpoint of the musician at his disposal: "Then without difficulty I could write a two-voiced melody that consists of two lines, two series of tones and notes that correspond to and complement each other, but which simultaneously are antagonistic and circumscribe each other." This stylistic predicament preoccupied Hesse incessantly during the next years. "This is my dilemma and my problem," the essay ends. "I shall never succeed in bending the two poles of life together, in writing down the double-voice of life's melody."

The Nuremberg Journey, which records the author's impressions during a lecture tour, is another step forward in the development of that fine sense of irony that Thomas Mann and André Gide admired in Hesse's later works. "If, under the increasing pressure of my life, I retreat into humor and view so-called reality from the fool's point of view," it is nothing but "an attempt to bridge the gap between Ideal and Experience." The lecture tour brought him into constant contact with other people, "realists," who regarded the writer as little more than a spectacle to be stared at and had little or no understanding for the meaning of his works. If this breakdown of communication was inevitable, then it was no longer necessary to restrict himself to the relatively simple forms that he had usually employed in his works. This experience explains the cavalier playfulness of form that characterizes most of his subsequent works.

After 1925 Hesse began to spend his winters in Zürich. He has repeatedly documented his complete lack of sympathy with technological civilization in all its manifestations. "I don't believe in our science," he observed in 1930, "nor in our politics, nor in our way of thinking, believing, amusing ourselves. I don't share a single one of the ideals of our age." This is more than the grumbling of a crabby reactionary. By "the ideals of our age" Hesse implies the blind materialistic faith in technology that Rilke and D. H. Lawrence decried. At the same time, with his customary frankness in self-evaluation, Hesse was quick to admit that his disavowal was largely the result of his own instinctive insecurity in the world of reality. In the afterword to the volume of poems *Crisis* he reasoned: "A great part, yes, the greatest part of the darker, perhaps deeper half of life was unconsciously passed over or prettified in my earlier writings. The reason for this lay, I believe, not in a naive repression of the sensual, but in a feeling of inferiority in that area. I was much more at home in the Spirit, in its broadest sense, than in the Senses." This is the situation that Hesse portrays in his next novel. *The Steppenwolf* (1927) is, par excellence, the novel of intellect in despair. Its hero is an intellectual who loses faith in the ideals of the spirit and regains it, ironically, by learning to affirm the senses and the world of trivial everyday that he had previously feared and rejected.

Structurally *The Steppenwolf* is the most daring of Hesse's works—as bold, Thomas Mann felt, as Joyce's *Ulysses* and Gide's *The Counterfeiters*. Experimentation for Hesse, however, means only the reshaping of traditional forms, not the contrivance of totally new structures. In its form the novel is closer to the realistic fairy tales of E. T. A. Hoffmann than to most modern novels. It was Hoffmann who transplanted the fairy tale from the gloomy Teutonic forests into the cities of his own time. They are "fairy tales" (*Märchen*) because they reproduce inner visions on the same level of authenticity as everyday occurrences. And that is the structural principle of Hesse's novel, which attempts to render the "double-voiced melody" of which he spoke in the essay *At the Spa*. All the action is recorded with the same degree of realism. The phantasmagoric effect is produced, as in Kafka's works, by the fact that many of these events are actually imaginary. The escalation from reality to imagination is so subtle that the line between reality and ideal is effaced; the reader must interpret every event on two levels; the double-voiced melody is achieved.

Harry Haller is a forty-eight-year-old intellectual who is able to bear his despair only because he has promised himself the luxury of suicide on his fiftieth birthday. It is scarcely necessary to recount the reasons for his despondency; Hesse has motivated his hero with intimately personal details. Separated from his wife, alienated from his friends for ideological reasons, suffering from poor eyesight and sciatica, and grievously alarmed by the glaring discrepancy between the ideals of his library and the reality of daily life, Haller is a photocopy of Hesse with one great exception: he has no sense of humor.

The fictitious autobiography, which begins at the nadir of Haller's despair, records the events of a crucial month in his life. Haller has devoted himself wholly to the Spirit, to the "Immortals" (Goethe, Novalis, Mozart), to "the golden trace" that gives life its meaning. We meet him just at a time when certain incidents have raised grave doubts in his mind. "Were those things that we called 'Culture,' that we called 'Spirit,' that we called 'Soul' and 'beautiful' and 'sacred'—were those things merely a spectre, already long dead and still considered genuine and alive only by a few fools like me?" Around this time he obtains a mysterious document entitled the "Tract of the Steppenwolf," which throws a new light on his dilemma. Haller has prided himself on being an outsider, a wolf from the steppes, cut off from bourgeois society and its values. The tract suggests that his misery actually stems from his failure to overcome many bourgeois inhibitions. Far from being an objective and serene outsider, like the true Immortals, he is wholly bourgeois in his instinctive fear of prostitutes, in his antipathy toward the jazz culture of his times. The Immortals that he worships were by no means men who rejected reality: their vision incorporated and transcended it; Goethe and Mozart were not only sublime geniuses, but very much men of their times. Ordinary mortals like Haller, who are incapable of sustaining the icy isolation of the Immortals, can contend with everyday reality by learning to laugh at it and by striving to recognize the "golden trace" even in the most trivial events of everyday life.

Quite by chance Haller is thrown into contact with this demimonde that he has previously avoided. To his amazement he discovers that he is able to enjoy the dancing, the idle chatter, the love-making of the prostitute Hermine, the musician Pablo, and their friends. In their conversations he gradually begins to hear echoed the voices and thoughts of the Immortals.

But the line between reality and ideal becomes tenuous. It is by no means clear—to Haller or to the reader—whether this wisdom actually comes from Hermine and Pablo or whether Haller himself is projecting these thoughts into otherwise trivial conversations and occurrences. In any case, the result is the same: Haller begins to recapture, during the month of his sensual apprenticeship, a new sense for the values of life.

His spiritual re-education culminates in the scenes of the Magic Theater, a narcotic phantasy induced by Pablo's drugs after a masquerade ball that Haller attends with Hermine. Here he visualizes himself in dozens of situations that he had previously rejected indignantly. He perceives, with the vividness of reality, that his rigid categories have completely collapsed, for he is theoretically capable of committing—and enjoying!—every human act from the basest to the noblest. This total acceptance of being characterizes the Immortals, but it involves a dreadful freedom that Haller is unable to sustain without the stimulation of drugs. When he grows sober in the early hours of the morning, he slips back into his old dualistic patterns and displays a fit of murderous jealousy when he finds Hermine in Pablo's arms. In his final vision Harry is confronted by a jury of the Immortals to whom he had aspired. For his failure, for his confusion of the Magic Theater with mundane reality, he is condemned to remain in the world until he learns to laugh at the discordant aspects of life, until he perceives—in other words—the symbolic identity of Mozart and Pablo.

The Steppenwolf is less symmetrically structured than the classicistic *Siddhartha*, but its organization, which bears detailed comparison to that of the sonata, is just as tight. (The musical analogy is not gratuitous. In this novel, which on both levels of reality—Mozart and Pablo—deals with music and musicians, Hesse was consciously exploiting a musical form.) Rather than force the book to a balanced conclusion, Hesse leaves Haller suspended at the end. "Pablo was waiting for me, Mozart was waiting for me." He is still very much enmeshed in the world of reality, but he faces it now with the consolation of humor and without the pathos of rigid intellectualism. The novel reflects the triadic rhythm of humanization that Hesse outlined in the important essay "A Bit of Theology" (1932). From an initial state of childlike innocence, thinking men graduate to a second level: knowledge of good and evil. Confronted there with the disparity between the Real and the Ideal, they are either crushed by despair or they struggle through to a third stage: a higher innocence beyond good and evil, or faith. This *principium individuationis* underlies almost all of Hesse's fiction. But here Hesse describes not an ideal process of individuation, as he did in *Siddhartha*, but a more realistic one. For most mortals, Hesse concludes, never attain the third level permanently; having glimpsed it, they continue like Haller to teeter precariously on the boundary between the world of men and the realm of the Immortals.

The Steppenwolf repelled many readers, who failed to see that the book is not a glorification of sex, jazz, and drug addiction, but a search for the eternal in the transitory, the divine in the mundane, the Immortals in the Jazz Era. His next novel was a more popular success. As early as 1908 Hesse wrote several chapters of a novel entitled *Bertold*, the story of a renegade seminarian in seventeenth-century Cologne who breaks his vows, murders, and escapes into the world of sensual adventure. Though the work remained a fragment, for many years the figure of the hero kept running through his mind—the renegade monk as another exemplification of the obsessive dualism between spirit and nature. When he started work, in 1928, on the novel *Narziss and Goldmund*, he took up the old plan again, moving it to the fifteenth century and shifting the original emphasis somewhat. Instead of allowing the conflict to take place within the soul of a single hero, as in *Demian* and *The Steppenwolf*, he conceived a *Doppelroman* (double novel) after the fashion of romantic writers such as Jean Paul and E. T. A. Hoffmann, in which the two attitudes are embodied symbolically in two different heroes: Narziss the priest, who rises to the position of abbot, personifies pure spirit sealed off from the world by the walls of his monastery; and Goldmund, Golden Mouth, Chrysostomus, the renegade monk who runs away from the monastery to seek life, woman, and ultimately art, embodies the world of nature and the senses.

As in *Siddhartha* the two worlds are separated spatially: the monastery is the preserve of spirit, and the wide world outside the realm of nature. The book itself falls into other overobvious structural divisions that occur when Hesse tries too hard to objectify his feelings. The first six chapters, during which Narziss helps Goldmund to discover that he is not cut out for the life of a celibate, take place in Mariabronn (where Hesse has described his own school Maulbronn). During the ten central chapters, in which Goldmund brawls his way through the world—making love to countless women, witnessing war, murder, pillage, rape, and becoming a gifted woodcarver—Narziss disappears wholly from the scene. In the last four chapters, reappearing like a *deus ex machina* to rescue Goldmund from prison and execution, the priest leads him back to the monastery, where the restless artist soon dies.

The original picaresque narrative of the ten middle chapters is a rather lively adventure story, and its erotic titillations account for at least part of its popularity. But the book bogs downs in ponderous, almost embarrassing symbolism. "Your home is the earth [Narziss tells his friend early in the novel], and ours is the idea. Your danger is to drown in the world of the senses, and ours it is to suffocate in airless space. You are an artist; I am a thinker: You sleep at the mother's breast while I lie awake in the desert. The sun shines for me, for you the moon and the stars. Your dreams are of girls, mine of boys. . . ." We might excuse one such passage, but similar ones recur throughout the novel. At the end Goldmund has become a physical wreck with features etched by the trials of the world whereas Narziss, hermetically sealed off in his monastery, has remained unravaged by time. Goldmund emerges triumphant since, as an artist, he has found the means to overcome time. His art, he tells Narziss, represents "the overcoming of transitoriness. I saw that something remained and outlived the fool's game and the death-dance of men: the works of art." The very security of his existence has cut Narziss off from those things that give life its meaning. Goldmund has been worn out by the world, but he has achieved a contentedness denied to his friend. For Life is epitomized not by the spiritual Father-image of the monastery, but by the elusive figure of the Mother that Goldmund pursues—a symbol reminiscent of Mother Eva in *Demian*. Goldmund realizes that this archetypal Mother represents not only love and life: "one could also call her a grave and decay. . . . She was the source of bliss and the source of death . . . in her, love and cruelty were one." In pursuit of Life, Goldmund ends up with the realization that this ultimate symbol encompasses all reality—a knowledge, he implies rather smugly, that has been denied Narziss with his monomaniacal preoccupation with the "paternal" spirit. "How will you die, Narziss, if you have no mother? Without a mother one cannot love. Without a mother one cannot die." Since Goldmund himself dies before he can complete his final masterpiece—the carving of "the great Eve-Mother"—he cannot transmit his vision to the world.

The artist gains an intuitive cognition denied to the intellectual, but is prevented from revealing it in its ultimate form.

Narziss and Goldmund, which was published in 1930, appeased those readers who prefer philosophy served up in spicy packages to the agonizing honesty and incisive analysis of books like *The Steppenwolf*. But the novel has almost an anachronistic effect. With its heavy-handed symbolism, its Jungian mother-figure, its labored dichotomy of "two worlds," and its total lack of humor, *Narziss and Goldmund* seems to be a regression to the period of *Demian;* it has little in common with the more sophisticated Hesse of *The Steppenwolf* and later works.

In 1931 Hesse married for a third time and moved with his wife into a new house in Montagnola. His happiness is reflected in *The Journey to the East* (1932), a highly private symbolic autobiography. In contrast to the studied earnestness of *Narziss and Goldmund*, the tone of *The Journey to the East* is ironic from the title on—an irony that André Gide emphasized in his preface to the French translation. The title is ironic because the narrator, H. H., never succeeds in telling us about his journey. Ten years earlier, in the period "after the Great War," H. H. had joined the League of Eastern Wayfarers in order to participate in a great pilgrimage to the East. But early in the journey the servant Leo disappeared, and this seemingly trivial occurrence created such dissension in the ranks that all members deserted one by one. When H. H. tries to write the history of the League, he discovers that he remembers only superficial details: its spirit has escaped him completely. What if the Order had not disintegrated around him? he muses. What if he himself had unwittingly deserted the League? He succeeds in finding Leo, whose harmonious existence contrasts sharply with H. H.'s own wretchedness. Leo assures H. H. that the Order is still intact and leads him to its archives so that H. H. can finish his history of the journey. In the archives H. H. learns that the humble servant Leo is in reality the Superior of the Order, that he incorporates its ideal of humble service. He himself, H. H., had been so much obsessed with his own individuality that he had neglected the first rule of the Order—service—and thus had become apostate to the Order. Once he realizes his error, he is punished by being smiled at by the assembled members and is then reaccepted into their ranks on the third level of Hesse's *principium individuationis*, where individuality, being assured, gives way to the higher ideal of service.

Apart from service, one of the central themes of the story is the idea that those who implicitly believe in an eternal realm of the spirit understand it intuitively; but its secret can never be communicated to those who do not believe in it. As a result, from the moment when H. H. deserts the League, he is no longer able to comprehend its journey. And at the end, when he is absorbed once more into the spiritual order, he is no longer able to communicate his experience to the noninitiate reader. The "journey" of the title takes place before and after the narration. The act of narration itself is actually a gesture of the narrator's despair since any true member of the League realizes the futility of trying to communicate the essential secret of the Order. Because Hesse succeeds in expressing all of this through the words of his narrator, who only gradually becomes aware of his own position, the tone of the narrative assumes a delightful irony that offsets the underlying mood of despair.

To lend form to a story that, by its very theme, might easily collapse into a formless jumble, Hesse employs—again ironically, as was the case with the Biblical prefiguration in *Demian*—a conventional framework. Down to the most astonishing details of plot and description his League and its leader Leo have characteristics borrowed from the Gothic romance of the late eighteenth century. The physical apparatus of the League's castle, the appearance of the "genius" of the League, the apprenticeship of the novice (H. H.)—all these features can be easily identified.

At the same time the whole narrative is a cunningly contrived symbolic autobiography. All the places mentioned, many of the incidents, and most of the characters (who are introduced under sobriquets) represent stages and events in Hesse's own life. Thus the Chinese Temple refers to the home of a friend in Wintherthur; "Ninon, known as 'the foreigner' " is a grammatical play on the maiden name of his own wife (Ninon Ausländer); and the rubric *Chattorum r. gest.* in the archives refers to the name that Hesse bore as a Latin student at Göppingen (Chattus) and to his subsequent deeds (*res gestae*). It is the most private book that Hesse wrote; every line contains allusions accessible only to the initiate. Yet the general meaning is obvious even to those who have never read another work by Hesse.

The "East" of the title is not, of course, a geographical specification; as early as 1911 Hesse had learned that the Orient is no longer a paradise for modern man. Rather, the title indicates a realm of spirit variously defined, in the course of the story, as a "psychocracy," a "unification of all times," and as a "melee of life and poetry." In this Eastern Kingdom one is "free to exchange inner and outer reality playfully" and "to shift time and space like stage sets." What we have is a symbolic representation of the Magical Thinking of *In Sight of Chaos*. But the tone, rather than being apocalyptically severe as there, is serenely playful. In the magical atmosphere of the story it is perfectly possible for H. H. to visit a celebration attended by figures from his own works (Pablo, Lauscher), by writers and musicians of the historical past (Hugo Wolf,

Brentano), and by living friends from Hesse's own present of 1931 (Hans C., Max and Tilli, Ninon). And all these characters are presented on the same level of fictional reality; there is absolutely no difference, here, between reality and ideal.

The idyll *Hours in the Garden* (1936) describes how Hesse himself, working among his flowers, liked to let his thoughts wander far afield, pulling together in the most startling combinations ideas or figures from the cultural tradition of the world. In *The Journey to the East* he has given a charming fictional form to this pastime. But by 1936 he had found a new name for this "*unio mystica* of all disparate elements of the *Universitas Litterarum*." He now called it the Glass Bead Game.

Hesse's last novel had a longer and more complicated genesis than his other books. Composed over a period of some eleven years, it was originally to have been the story of "a man who, in several reincarnations, experiences the great epochs in the history of humanity"—a series of parallel lives beginning in prehistoric times, running through the Golden Age of India, the patristic period of early Christianity and eighteenth-century Pietism in Germany, and ending in a pedagogical province in the future. But gradually Hesse's intentions shifted. By 1938 he had decided to focus his main attention on the final stage—Joseph Knecht in the Castalia of 2400. The other episodes were retained, but incorporated in the novel as school exercises written by young Knecht.

The pedagogical province of Castalia was originally envisaged as another variation on the Journey to the East—the representation of an ideal kingdom of the spirit, centered upon the Glass Bead Game, which is "a refined, symbolic form of the search for perfection, a sublime alchemy, an approach to the spirit that is unified in itself beyond all images." But by 1938 two great influences had altered Hesse's thinking.

First, his study of the historical writings of Jacob Burckhardt—the Pater Jacobus of his novel—made him aware of the relativism of all historical organisms, including even such an idealized society as Castalia. He was no longer able to posit Castalia as an absolute ideal, valid for all times and under all circumstances. Second, the horrors of Nazism in Germany had opened his eyes to the futility of purely aesthetic ideals in the world of reality: like many of his contemporaries he became convinced of the necessity for the existential engagement of the individual. Thus *The Glass Bead Game*, which was begun in 1931 as a hymn to the aesthetic kingdom of the spirit, became by the time of its publication in 1943 a repudiation of disengagement in favor of personal commitment. In this sense Hesse's novel, like Hermann Broch's *The Death of Vergil*, is a compelling document of the transition from the aestheticism of the early twentieth century to the *littérature engagée* of our own times.

Structurally the novel falls into three parts (as do most of his later novels). A long introduction sketches the history of the Glass Bead Game up to the time of Joseph Knecht and outlines the organization of the pedagogical province. The poems and fictitious lives written by Knecht while he was a student are reproduced in a bulky appendix. The twelve central chapters, which follow the pattern of the traditional German *Bildungsroman*, trace the story of Knecht's development from his boyhood in the preparatory schools of Castalia through his rise to the top of the Order and, finally, his abdication. The world of *The Glass Bead Game*, in radical contradistinction to Hesse's other novels, is not polar—Nature and Spirit—but divided into three "powers" suggested to Hesse by his reading of Burckhardt: Church, State, and Culture. Young Knecht grows up in the province of Culture. It is only when he is sent as a representative of Castalia to the monastery of

Mariafels, where he spends two years in the company of Pater Jacobus, that he begins for the first time to question the validity of an Order devoted exclusively to the cultivation of the spirit. Aroused by his debates with Pater Jacobus, Knecht rapidly recognizes the dangers inherent in the pedagogical province. In his best friend, the musician Tegularius, he witnesses the ravages of a brilliant mind that devolves with constant narcissism upon itself. During his eight years as Magister Ludi, the supreme title in the hierarchy of Castalia, Knecht preserves this sense of historicism that affords him a certain ironic distance from the games that he performs with an unmatched virtuosity.

Knecht realizes that Castalia is heading toward collapse; an art wholly divorced from life and moral commitment is suicidal. In order to make a gesture of his alarm, Knecht decides to defect and go into the world, where he intends to devote himself to the service of men. (*Knecht* means "servant" in German.) Discarding disengagement, he takes upon himself the responsibility of action and volunteers to tutor the son of his worldly friend Plinio Designori. Just as Art must perish without Life, Life becomes brutish without Culture. Since the official realms of State and Culture have lost virtually all contact, existing side by side in a state of mutual contempt, only responsible individuals like Knecht can mediate between them. On the third morning of his defection, however, Knecht's sense of personal commitment causes his death. His young pupil Tito plunges into the icy waters of a mountain lake for a swim, and Knecht, reluctant at such an early point in their relationship to betray any lack of solidarity, follows him into the water and drowns. A great deal has been written about the symbolic overtones of Knecht's death, but Hesse has made the basic meaning quite explicit. "Knecht could have refrained, finely and intelligently, from leaping into the mountain water despite his illness," he wrote in 1947. "Yet he does it all the same because there is in him something stronger than intelligence, because he cannot disappoint this boy who is so difficult to win over. And he leaves behind a Tito for whom this sacrificial death of a man vastly superior to him will remain forever an admonition and an example."

Yet the true beneficiary of Knecht's death is not Tito, or anyone else living at the time of Knecht, but rather the generation represented by the anonymous narrator, who writes some years after Knecht's death. This narrator describes the Castalia of the past, the pedagogical province devoted exclusively to the cultivation of spirit in the abstract, with the irony that we have grown accustomed to expect from Hesse. The later Castalia in which he lives is one that has profited from Knecht's criticism and Knecht's example; it is a Castalia far removed from pure aestheticism, a realm of Culture that exists in a tension of interaction with State and Religion.

Hesse has moved away from the position of pure contemplation that seemed to constitute his ideal in the 'twenties and early 'thirties. In the terms of the novel he is striving for a synthesis of the *vita activa* and the *vita contemplativa*. In Castalia the ideal is symbolized by music, which requires a constant compromise between practice and theory, the abstract and the concrete, the spiritual and the sensual. For this reason the old Magister Musicae, more than any of the brilliant constellation of mandarins in Castalia, anticipates Knecht's final resolution and decision. Hesse's last novel is in no way a depiction of the charms of disengagement, but rather a plea for human commitment and for an art nourished by life, for a life enriched by art.

The Glass Bead Game was Hesse's last novel. Plagued by increasingly poor eyesight, by the leukemia that precipitated his death in 1962, by the entreaties of hundreds of correspondents, and by the other demands upon literary figures of world renown, he barricaded himself in Montagnola behind a sign reading "No Visitors Please." Yet during these last twenty years his literary production continued at an astonishing pace. Apart from hundreds of private letters, Hesse wrote a number of stories, autobiographical reflections, circular letters to his friends, and poems that fill several volumes. In these last works Hesse's attitude has been distilled into what might be called the classicism of revolt. Under the deceptively simple surfaces of landscape descriptions, childhood reminiscences, or episodes from the daily life of a septuagenarian we find the same preoccupation with the themes that characterize his works from 1917 on. "All my works," he suggested in 1954, "can be interpreted as a defense (sometimes also an anguished cry) of the individual." In this late prose it is not the attitude that has changed, but the tone. German scholars are fond of speaking of the *Altersstil*—the style of old age—of their writers: the brittle, symbolic, classically reduced and often ironic style that is pronounced, for instance, in the late works of Goethe or Thomas Mann. There is no better example of this *Altersstil* than Hesse's late prose, which has shed the pathos of individualism to immerse itself wholly in its object.

Hesse's growth as a writer parallels the development of literature in the twentieth century from aestheticism to engagement. But he was always an amused observer, never a member of movements or a frantic participant in the contest to keep abreast of the times. He was drawn to themes that are perhaps more urgent today than in ages with accepted patterns of belief, but still universal: the quest for identity, the search for personal values, the impulse to moral commitment. Just as he was reluctant to concern himself with issues that are merely timely, he also refused to engage in pure innovation and stylistic experimentation. Even in the least conventional of his novels he simply reshapes existing forms. It is his achievement to have shown to what extent modernity is traditional, in its thought and in its form; his works bridge the gap, so to speak, between romanticism and existentialism. His range was narrow and his expression essentially lyrical, for he rarely went beyond himself. At most, after 1917, he transposed his themes from the minor key of the private to the major key of the symbolic. For this reason Hesse does not rank, as a novelist, with Proust, Joyce, or Thomas Mann; and in his poetry he never approached Rilke, Eliot, or Valéry. But in the realm of poetic fiction—a province marked out by his favorite romantic authors and explored by Rilke, Hermann Broch, Virginia Woolf, André Gide, and others—his best works are unsurpassed. Sometimes, in this difficult terrain, he stumbled through a landscape cluttered with thickets of allegory. But with *The Steppenwolf*, *The Journey to the East*, and *The Glass Bead Game* he added lasting names to the map of our poetic imagination.

SELECTED BIBLIOGRAPHY

PRINCIPAL WORKS OF HERMANN HESSE

NOTE: *The standard edition of Hesse's works comprises seven volumes of* Gesammelte Schriften *published by Suhrkamp Verlag in Frankfurt am Main. This bibliography lists the most important works by first edition as well as the most recent English translation, if any. (Harper & Row is currently republishing Hesse's novels in new translations.)*

Romantische Lieder. Dresden, Pierson, 1899.
Eine Stunde hinter Mitternacht. Leipzig, Diederichs, 1899.
Hinterlassene Schriften und Gedichte von Hermann Lauscher. Basel, Reich, 1901.
Peter Camenzind. Berlin, Fischer, 1904. (Peter Camenzind. Tr. Walter J. Strachan. London, Owen, 1961.)

Unterm Rad. Berlin, Fischer, 1906. (The Prodigy. Tr. Walter J. Strachan. London, Owen, 1957.)
Diesseits. Berlin, Fischer, 1907.
Nachbarn. Berlin, Fischer, 1909.
Gertrud. München, Langen, 1910. (Gertrude. Tr. Hilda Rosner. London, Owen, 1955.)
Aus Indien. Berlin, Fischer, 1913.
Rosshalde. Berlin, Fischer, 1914.
Knulp. Drei Geschichten aus dem Leben Knulps. Berlin, Fischer, 1915.
Demian. Die Geschichte einer Jugend von Emil Sinclair. Berlin, Fischer, 1919. (Demian. Tr. N. H. Priday [1923]. Reprinted with a preface by Thomas Mann: New York, Holt, 1948. Also tr. Michael Roloff and Michael Lebeck. New York, Harper & Row, 1965.)
Märchen. Berlin, Fischer, 1919.
Klingsors letzter Sommer. Berlin, Fischer, 1920. (Contains Klein und Wagner.)
Blick ins Chaos. Drei Aufsätze. Bern, Seldwyla, 1920. (In Sight of Chaos. Tr. Stephen Hudson. Zürich, Seldwyla, 1923.)
Siddhartha. Eine indische Dichtung. Berlin, Fischer, 1922. (Siddhartha. Tr. Hilda Rosner. New York, New Directions, 1957.)
Kurgast. Aufzeichnungen von einer Badener Kur. Berlin, Fischer, 1925.
Die Nürnberger Reise. Berlin, Fischer, 1927.
Der Steppenwolf. Berlin, Fischer, 1927. (The Steppenwolf. Tr. Basil Creighton [1929]. Revised by Joseph Mileck and Horst Frenz: New York, Holt, 1963.)
Betrachtungen. Berlin, Fischer, 1928.
Krisis. Ein Stück Tagebuch. Berlin, Fischer, 1928.
Narziss und Goldmund. Berlin, Fischer, 1930. (Death and the Lover. Tr. Geoffrey Dunlop [1932]. Reissued: New York, Praeger, 1959.)
Die Morgenlandfahrt. Berlin, Fischer, 1932. (The Journey to the East. Tr. Hilda Rosner. New York, Noonday Press, 1957.)
Stunden im Garten. Eine Idylle. Wien, Bermann-Fischer, 1936.
Gedichte. Zürich, Fretz und Wasmuth, 1942.
Das Glasperlenspiel. Versuch einer Lebensbeschreibung des Mägister Ludi Josef Knecht samt Knechts hinterlassenen Schriften. 2 vols. Zürich, Fretz und Wasmuth, 1943. (Magister Ludi. Tr. Mervyn Savill [1949]. Reissued: New York, Ungar, 1957.)
Krieg und Frieden. Betrachtungen zu Krieg und Politik seit dem Jahr 1914. Zürich, Fretz und Wasmuth, 1946.

Späte Prosa. Berlin, Suhrkamp, 1951.
Briefe. Berlin, Suhrkamp, 1951. Enlarged edition: Frankfurt am Main, Suhrkamp, 1964.
Prosa aus dem Nachlass. Ed. Ninon Hesse. Frankfurt am Main, Suhrkamp, 1965.

CRITICAL WORKS AND COMMENTARY

Ball, Hugo. Hermann Hesse. Sein Leben und sein Werk [1927]. Mit einem Anhang von Anni Carlsson. Berlin, Suhrkamp, 1947.
Baumer, Franz. Hermann Hesse. Berlin, Colloqium, 1959.
Engel, Eva J. "Hermann Hesse," in German Men of Letters. Ed. Alex Natan. Vol. II, London, Wolff, 1963, pp. 249–74.
Freedman, Ralph. The Lyrical Novel. Studies in Hermann Hesse, André Gide, and Virginia Woolf. Princeton, N. J., Princeton University Press, 1963, pp. 42–118.
Mileck, Joseph. Hermann Hesse and His Critics. The Criticism and Bibliography of Half a Century. Chapel Hill, N. C., University of North Carolina Press, 1958.
Rose, Ernst. Faith from the Abyss: Hermann Hesse's Way from Romanticism to Modernity. New York, New York University Press, 1965.
Waibler, Helmut. Hermann Hesse. Eine Bibliographie. Bern & München, Francke, 1962.
Zeller, Bernard. Hermann Hesse. Eine Chronik in Bildern. Frankfurt am Main, Suhrkamp, 1960.
———. Hermann Hesse in Selbstzeugnissen und Bilddokumenten. Reinbek bei Hamburg, Rowohlt, 1963.
Ziolkowski, Theodore. The Novels of Hermann Hesse. A Study in Theme and Structure. Princeton, N. J., Princeton University Press, 1965.